Headline Series

No. 276   FOREIGN POLICY ASSOCIATION $4.00

SINO-AMERICAN RELATIONS AFTER NORMALIZATION
Toward the Second Decade

by Steven M. Goldstein and Jay Mathews

Introduction 3

1
Toward a New Consensus: 1978–1986 9

2
Strategic Triangle:
The Impact of Sino-Soviet Relations 17

3
The Taiwan Issue 24

4
Economic Relations 31

5
China's Reform Process 41

6
The Future of the Relationship 54

Talking It Over 61

Cover Design: Hersch Wartik

The Authors

STEVEN M. GOLDSTEIN received his Ph.D. in political science from Columbia University. In 1968 he joined the faculty at Smith College, where he is now professor and chairman of the Department of Government. He has also taught at the Fletcher School of Law and Diplomacy and Columbia University. His writings have dealt with a broad range of contemporary Chinese political topics, including peasant revolution and elite politics. However, his major field of interest is Chinese foreign policy, particularly Sino-American relations.

Photo by Lisa Bodeur.

JAY MATHEWS is the Western bureau chief of *The Washington Post*. From 1976 to 1979 he was *The Washington Post* bureau chief in Hong Kong. He then moved to Beijing in 1979 to become his newspaper's first resident correspondent in China, remaining there through 1980. He and his wife, Linda Mathews, a *Los Angeles Times* correspondent, coauthored *One Billion: A China Chronicle* (Random House, 1983). Mr. Mathews received a master's degree in East Asian Studies from Harvard University. He served with the U.S. Army in Vietnam and recently won the National Education Reporting Award.

The Foreign Policy Association

The Foreign Policy Association is a private, nonprofit, nonpartisan educational organization. Its purpose is to stimulate wider interest and more effective participation in, and greater understanding of, world affairs among American citizens. Among its activities is the continuous publication, dating from 1935, of the HEADLINE SERIES. The authors are responsible for factual accuracy and for the views expressed. FPA itself takes no position on issues of U.S. foreign policy.

HEADLINE SERIES (ISSN 0017-8780) is published five times a year, January, March, May, September and November, by the Foreign Policy Association, Inc., 205 Lexington Ave., New York, N.Y. 10016. Chairman, Robert V. Lindsay; President, Archie E. Albright; Editor, Nancy L. Hoepli; Senior Editor, Ann R. Monjo; Associate Editor, K. M. Rohan. Subscription rates, $15.00 for 5 issues; $25.00 for 10 issues; $30.00 for 15 issues. Single copy price $4.00. Discount 25% on 10 to 99 copies; 30% on 100 to 499; 35% on 500 to 999; 40% on 1,000 or more. Payment must accompany order for $8 or less. Add $1 for postage. Second-class postage paid at New York, N.Y. POSTMASTER: Send address changes to HEADLINE SERIES, Foreign Policy Association, 205 Lexington Ave., New York, N.Y. 10016. Copyright 1986 by Foreign Policy Association, Inc. Composed and printed at Science Press, Ephrata, Pa.

Library of Congress Catalog Card No. 86-81093
ISBN 0-87124-105-6

美國

Introduction

Nearly half a century ago, Americans began dealing with the men and women who were to shape today's China. A few American journalists, principally Edgar and Helen Foster Snow and Agnes Smedley, slipped past exasperated Nationalist Chinese and warlord armies in the mid-1930s to see the mysterious Chinese Communists firsthand. Mao Zedong and Zhu De were at that time little more than curiosities. They were the leaders of a rebel band that had miraculously survived a 6,000-mile trek from south-central China, where they had faced encirclement and defeat at the hands of Chiang Kai-shek's Nationalist (Kuomintang) forces. To their American visitors the Communists appeared honest and confident—qualities the Americans could find in none of the other contenders for political power.

When the Japanese opened a full-scale offensive in July 1937, the Communists and the Nationalists appealed for unity, but by 1941 China's two major parties were once again at the point of civil war. When the United States entered the war in the Pacific following the Japanese attack on Pearl Harbor, it implicitly took the Nationalist side by continuing to recognize Chiang's government as the legitimate ruling force in China. Still, over Chiang's objections, the United States tried to take advantage of the obvious

The publication of this issue of the HEADLINE SERIES *was made possible, in part, by the China Council of The Asia Society.*

military potential of the Communists. In 1944, an official U.S. delegation visited Mao's forces in Yenan. The Americans were greeted warmly. The Communist leaders spoke of future relations with Washington. The diplomats and military officers, like the earlier journalists, were impressed by the vigor and nationalism of the Communists. Many returned forecasting the stunning victory that Mao's forces did, in fact, achieve four years after the war's end.

Imaginative historians have argued that the United States could have spared itself decades of wasteful estrangement from China by accommodating the Communists and detaching itself from the Kuomintang. This argument assumes that the leaders of the United States and China had the political maneuvering room to make such a bargain. This is a very doubtful assumption. The post-1945 world was very different from what it had been even a year earlier. The Chinese Communist party (CCP) was fighting a revolutionary war. Mao could not justify radical changes in the national economy without attacking Western economic interests and their free-enterprise remnants in Shanghai, Canton and other coastal cities. He could not prove that he was a genuine nationalist unless he ejected the foreign presence. Finally, as the world entered the cold-war era, China's Communists could not risk a quarrel with Soviet dictator Joseph Stalin, a very uncertain ally during the perilous infancy of their new regime. They needed the Soviet Union's economic assistance and security umbrella.

Looking at the other side of the Pacific, no American government would have been willing to pay the political price of dealing with the relentlessly anti-Western Chinese Communists. U.S. efforts to contain Communist influence in Europe inhibited any inclination to deal differently with Marxists in Asia.

On October 1, 1949, Mao walked onto a platform atop the old imperial Tiananmen (Gate of Heavenly Peace) in Beijing (Peking) and declared that China had "stood up." In Taiwan, Chiang was eliminating pockets of resistance to the Nationalist takeover of that offshore island, an echo of what the Communists were doing to Nationalist sympathizers and other perceived reactionaries on the mainland.

As the civil war ended in China, Harry S. Truman's Administration, preferring to let the dust settle on the mainland, avoided ties with the remnants of the Nationalist regime. The United States hoped to work out some relationship with China's new rulers. When Kim Il Sung's North Korean forces invaded South Korea in June 1950, however, the chances of Sino-American rapprochement were destroyed. As the American Seventh Fleet moved into the Taiwan Strait, the Chinese began a virulent campaign to aid North Korea and oppose the United States. General Douglas MacArthur, misreading Chinese resolve, pushed close to the Chinese border and the Communist leadership, sensing a new American intervention in China's affairs, sent in "volunteer troops." Chinese and Americans were soon killing each other. Any hope of amicable Sino-American relations was buried in the frozen mud of the Korean peninsula.

Throughout the 1950s and 1960s, movement toward better relations made little progress. The two countries were out of sync. During the mid-1950s, after the Korean War, China made some overtures to Washington, but they were rejected by Secretary of State John Foster Dulles. The Administration supported Chiang Kai-shek's Nationalists who had fled to Taiwan, and it did everything possible to isolate the People's Republic of China and keep it out of the community of nations. Washington refused to consider trade with China and strongly discouraged its allies from doing so. The United States poured economic and military aid into Taiwan, buttressing Chiang's claim that he, and not the mainland government, spoke for the Chinese people.

In the early 1960s, President John F. Kennedy considered opening a dialogue with China. But Beijing's increasingly anti-imperialist rhetoric and its attacks on the Soviet Union for its policy of détente with the United States doomed Washington's initiatives to failure. With American involvement in the Vietnam war, the Sino-American split widened. American policymakers spoke openly of a Chinese threat to Southeast Asia.

China sent military support to Vietnam and, at times, seemed on the verge of intervention. However, during much of the Vietnam war China was preoccupied with domestic problems. In

1966, seeing signs that the socialist revolution was degenerating and resentful of his Politburo colleagues' readiness to nudge him aside, Mao launched the Cultural Revolution. By calling on the people to revolt against those in power who were "taking the capitalist road," Mao hoped to unseat his opponents and bring China back to his view of what socialism should be. Mass demonstrations and often violent factional politics brought the nation to a state of near anarchy.

Radical rhetoric and internal chaos left the nation weak and isolated in the world. In 1968 the Soviet Union invaded Czechoslovakia, claiming that it was Moscow's duty to do so since the country had ceased being socialist. Given past Soviet statements regarding the end of socialism in China, the armed conflict on the Sino-Soviet border in early 1969 seemed ominous. Mao and his second in command, Zhou Enlai, realized that China had to end its isolation. The moment seemed right to reevaluate China's relationship with the United States. China sent subtle signals to Washington suggesting an openness to renewed contact.

President Richard M. Nixon and his national security adviser, Henry A. Kissinger, read these signals correctly and reciprocated with a series of tension-easing gestures. The process reached its culmination when, during a visit to Pakistan in July 1971, Kissinger feigned illness, cancelled his appointments, and secretly flew to Beijing to arrange President Nixon's historic visit to China in February 1972.

The visit, covered on national television in the United States, rekindled American fascination with China. Two decades of animosity seemed to disappear overnight. More concretely, during the President's visit Nixon, Kissinger, Mao and Zhou completed the Shanghai Communiqué, a document that tried to reflect the common interests of the two nations even as it revealed their differences.

The major points of agreement were a common wish to normalize relations and a commitment to oppose "hegemony"— the code word for Soviet influence—in Asia. There followed separate statements in which the United States and China expressed their relative positions on the difficult Taiwan question. Although there had been little agreement on that issue, the American statement did acknowledge that Chinese on both sides of the Taiwan Strait "maintain there is but one China and that Taiwan is a part of China." Washington expressed its wish that the Taiwan question be resolved peacefully by the Chinese themselves and agreed to reduce its military forces in Taiwan as tension in the area decreased. The Chinese restated their position that the Taiwan issue was "the crucial question obstructing the normalization of relations between China and the United States." They insisted that the question was China's internal matter, rejecting as unacceptable any solution other than the island's return as a Chinese province.

During the years between the Shanghai Communiqué and the December 1978 agreement to normalize relations, Sino-American rapprochement lost some of its momentum. The two governments established liaison offices in Washington and Beijing in 1973, but they both had to face domestic instability. In the United States the Watergate affair, triggered by the break-in of Democratic party headquarters, paralyzed President Nixon's Administration and ultimately led to his resignation. In China, despite the return of many pre-Cultural Revolution figures, most prominently Deng Xiaoping, and the reversal of many of the policies of the immediate past, maneuvering started for succession to Chairman Mao. Radical opposition made the development of any substantive economic or cultural relationships with the United States difficult. During these years, exchanges were limited, trade fluctuated and, despite President Gerald R. Ford's trip to China in December 1975, relations made little headway.

By 1978, there had been considerable change in China. Mao died in September 1976, and a month later his radical supporters were purged. In mid-1977 Deng Xiaoping made his second political comeback and almost immediately began to put China on a more certain course. President Jimmy Carter's national security adviser, Zbigniew Brzezinski, traveled to Beijing in May 1978 and informed his hosts that President Carter had decided to normalize relations with China.

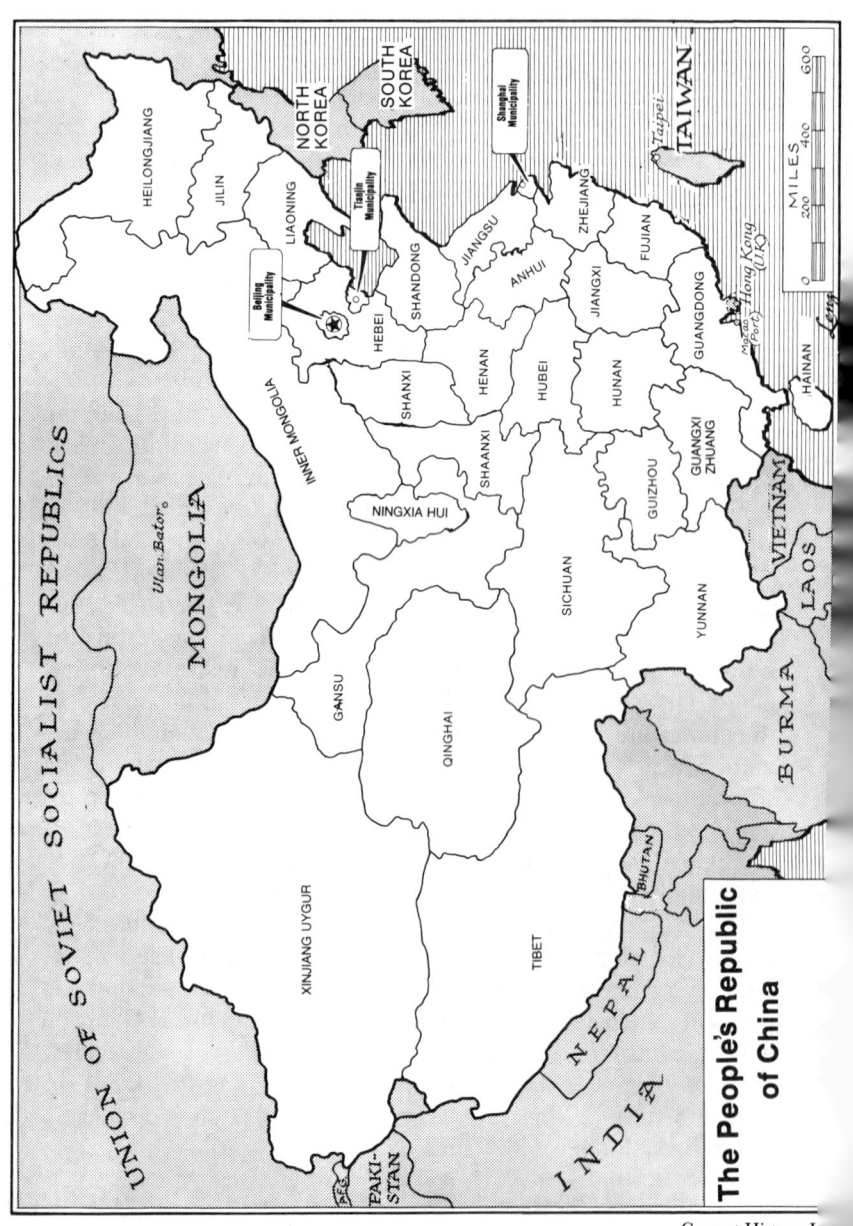

1

Toward a New Consensus: 1978–1986

With the benefit of seven years' hindsight, "normalization" seems a curious term to use to describe the evolution of Sino-American relations since 1978. The course of this evolution has been anything but normal. The consensus that formed the basis for mutual recognition in 1978 began to erode rather quickly. Relations between Washington and Beijing moved like a roller coaster through high points of congeniality and low points of near-rupture.

On the morning of December 16, 1978, in Beijing (the evening of December 15 in Washington), when the United States and China announced that they would grant each other full diplomatic recognition, the mood was one of great optimism. Leonard Woodcock would become a full-fledged American ambassador to China; the U.S. embassy in Taiwan would be closed; all American troops would leave the island; the United States would allow its security treaty with Taiwan to lapse after another year. Two weeks later it was announced that Vice Premier Deng Xiaoping would visit the United States. Taiwan remained the major sticking point, but that issue was "set aside" at the time of normalization.

The new era of Sino-American friendship began at the stroke of midnight on New Year's Eve. In less than a month Deng was in the United States, cutting a wide swath through the U.S. media. He donned a cowboy hat in Houston, Texas, and conducted a nationally televised prime-time press interview in Washington, leaving behind a wave of pro-Chinese sentiment. Deng had coyly sidestepped questions about the harsh treatment of domestic critics and continuing threats of a Chinese response to Vietnam's pro-Soviet tilt and invasion of Cambodia.

Very soon, however, the euphoria of the New Year began to erode. The Chinese invaded Vietnam on February 17, 1979. With the invasion came a swift crackdown on China's small but enthusiastic democracy movement. The wall-poster writers who expressed criticism of the regime had enjoyed little support among the Chinese, but their apparent freedom of speech had influenced the American view of China. Many Americans took another look at the amiable Deng.

China's economic difficulties—unemployment, malnutrition and a serious budget deficit—accelerated the decline in Sino-American goodwill, but the greatest strain in relations came, not surprisingly, at their most vulnerable point—Taiwan. In April 1979 President Carter signed the Taiwan Relations Act. In part a product of pro-Taiwan sympathy in Congress, the act spelled out a broad range of areas where relations with Taiwan would be maintained. Further, it announced that normalization with China had been based on the assumption that the Taiwan question would be solved peacefully, pledged to "maintain the capacity of the United States" to resist attempts to coerce Taiwan, declared that any attempt to use other than peaceful means would be viewed with "grave concern" by the United States, and pledged to provide Taiwan with "arms of a defensive character."

The Chinese were—and continue to be—angered by the Taiwan Relations Act. China had expected normalization to distance Washington from Taiwan and make the Nationalist government in Taipei, Taiwan's capital, more willing to talk to

Beijing. Instead, the Congress of the United States had given assistance to Taiwan a basis in American law. For the Chinese this represented a step back from normalization.

The mercurial quality of Sino-American relations in the first months of 1979 set the tone for the future. As would be the case several times again, it was an official visit that helped patch up some of the differences. Vice President Walter F. Mondale, in a speech at Beijing University in August 1979, the first ever by an American official to be broadcast nationwide, implicitly highlighted the two nations' common anti-Soviet interest. He assured his Chinese audience that "any nation which seeks to weaken or isolate you in world affairs assumes a stance counter to American interests."

Global politics gave the relationship a further boost. In December 1979 the Soviet Union invaded Afghanistan. When Secretary of Defense Harold Brown arrived in Beijing on a previously scheduled visit during the first week in January, the impact of Soviet actions was soon evident: Chinese and American defense specialists discussed concrete areas of cooperation.

Even as the foundation of the elusive strategic relationship between the United States and China was being laid, serious strains were appearing. The cause was again Taiwan. In the last year of the Carter Administration, Beijing saw growing signs of American regression on the Taiwan question. The Chinese characterized the continued U.S. sale of arms to Taiwan as "nothing but bad faith in international relations." They objected when the State Department granted clearance for talks between Taiwan and U.S. companies on the sale of the new FX jet fighters.

The Reagan candidacy made a bad situation worse. During the campaign Ronald Reagan suggested publicly that he would restore official relations with Taiwan. In 1981 Beijing increased its distance from what it viewed as an increasingly unreliable Washington.

During this same period, China took a fresh look at the Soviet Union. Chinese statements suggested that Beijing no longer saw the northern neighbor as an unchallenged, aggressive power.

Instead, Beijing saw a country beset by domestic economic difficulties, confronting a hostile Reagan Administration and preoccupied with dissension in Poland and conflict in Afghanistan. This diminished the Soviet threat to China and made the logic of China's alignment with the United States less compelling. Hu Yaobang, the Communist party chief, expressed Beijing's new "independent foreign policy" succinctly when he declared in 1982, "China never attaches itself to any big power or group of powers, and never yields to pressure from any big power."

Relations Hit New Low

The new Reagan Administration faced the dual problem of establishing its credibility with the Chinese while assessing China's new posture and framing an appropriate response. The transition to a new basis for Sino-American relations was anything but smooth.

On his trip to Beijing in June 1981, Secretary of State Alexander M. Haig Jr. insisted on Washington's right to supply weapons to Taiwan, but he tried to sugar the pill with a promise of weapons for China. At a press conference in Beijing he announced that China would be removed from the American list of nations denied lethal weapons.

As political scientist and Sinologist Jonathan Pollack of the Rand Corporation has noted, the Chinese were suspicious. Haig seemed to be attempting to gain China's acquiescence to a continued American relationship with Taiwan by dangling the promise of future arms. When Reagan announced at a press conference in Washington hours after Haig's in Beijing that the decision to supply China with weapons did not alter his policy or "feelings" toward Taiwan, the Chinese were furious.

The Haig visit was a diplomatic disaster. Rather than cementing the relationship with China or making the Chinese more understanding of Washington's position on Taiwan, it deepened Chinese distrust. It was only by the greatest restraint on both sides—and a series of concessions by the Reagan Administration—that a serious rupture was avoided.

The first concession came when Washington announced early

in 1982 that it would not be supplying the FX fighter plane to Taiwan, but that coproduction of the less sophisticated F-5E would continue. The Chinese seemed satisfied and indicated that they were "willing to negotiate with the United States for an end to sales within a time limit."

It was from these beginnings that the United States and China were able to fashion the joint communiqué that was released on August 17, 1982. In return for a Chinese statement that a peaceful settlement of the Taiwan issue was its "fundamental policy," the United States asserted that it did not "seek to carry out a long-term policy of arms sales to Taiwan," but rather "to reduce gradually its sales of arms to Taiwan, leading over a period of time to a final resolution." In the meantime, Washington pledged that "arms sales to Taiwan will not exceed, either in qualitative or quantitative terms, the level of those supplied...since the establishment of diplomatic relations...."

The communiqué did not meet Beijing's desire for a U.S. commitment to end arms sales to Taiwan "within a time limit." But from Beijing's perspective, the Reagan Administration's promise to reduce the flow of arms to Taiwan was significant and the agreement averted a crisis in Sino-American relations. Now the United States would have to make good on its pledges.

Building a New Relationship

Despite the communiqué, bilateral relations showed little improvement. The Chinese remained suspicious of American dalliances with Taiwan, were irate over a suit brought by American holders of imperial Chinese bonds, were decidedly dissatisfied over the pace of American technology transfer, and were unhappy over restrictions on Chinese textile exports.

It fell to Secretary of State George P. Shultz to discuss these questions when he visited China in February 1983. The Chinese laid out the full range of their grievances with the United States. Shultz responded with equal candor, but also with considerable calm. Shultz's businesslike style and his apparent appreciation of the importance of the economic issues in Sino-American relations were well received in Beijing.

Ironically, the quality of Sino-American relations after the Shultz visit did not improve significantly. Later in the month President Reagan again angered the Chinese with apparently pro-Taiwan comments. During the spring, relations were further aggravated by the granting of political asylum to the Chinese tennis player, Hu Na, Beijing's retaliatory cancellation of all sports and cultural exchanges, and the decision by Pan American to reconsider the resumption of commercial service to Taiwan.

Another major concession by the Reagan Administration seemed to turn relations around once again. Secretary of Commerce Malcolm Baldrige announced in May that the United States would take steps to liberalize its position on technology transfer. The following month Washington announced that China would be moved from group P to the group V export category, joining Egypt as a "friendly, nonallied" nation.

The American willingness to expedite technology transfer went a long way toward accommodating China's desire for a relationship based more on economic cooperation than on strategic considerations. During the summer the United States gave China a generous textile quota. In September the Chinese reciprocated by ending the boycott of American agricultural goods begun in response to the textile controversy.

By September Chinese leaders were talking openly of improved relations and plans to accelerate the pace of high-level visits. However, in keeping with its independent foreign policy, China would pursue its talks with the Soviet Union, would continue to criticize America's global policy when criticism seemed warranted, and, most importantly, would react harshly to any signs of retrogression on the Taiwan issue by the still-suspect Reagan Administration.

In the last months of 1983, two congressional decisions threatened the upcoming exchange of visits by President Reagan and Chinese Premier Zhao Ziyang. A Senate Foreign Relations Committee resolution called for the peaceful settlement of the Taiwan issue, and an amendment passed by both houses of Congress called for American support of Taiwan's continued full membership in the Asian Development Bank (ADB) should

Dana Summers, *The Orlando Sentinel.*

'Looks like President Li's visit to America went well.'

China be admitted. Through his spokesman, the President maintained that although he would sign the ADB bill, neither congressional statement represented national policy. A crisis was narrowly averted.

Relationship Outlined

Premier Zhao visited the United States in January 1984, and President Reagan returned the visit in April. In the course of these two visits, the outlines of a new Sino-American economic relationship developed, one that superseded the anti-Soviet consensus of the late 1970s.

During his January trip, Zhao spoke to two major American business audiences and delivered one simple message: China had opened the door to international economic cooperation and would not close it. President Reagan, who made a point of visiting a joint economic venture in Shanghai, spoke of himself as a salesman who would do everything to promote sales short of putting a "Buy American" sticker on his bag. The concrete results of both trips were largely economic: a pact on scientific and cultural exchanges, an agreement on taxation, and a nuclear cooperation agreement intended to pave the way for U.S. firms to participate in building Chinese nuclear reactors.

Although it had lost some of its earlier prominence, the strategic component remained an integral part of the relationship. President Reagan had come to appreciate China for its value in opposing the Soviet Union, and the two countries still shared a number of other important strategic concerns. China continued to seek stability on the Korean peninsula despite evidence of the growing displeasure of North Korean Communist leader Kim Il Sung. In Vietnam and in Thailand, U.S. and Chinese policies followed largely parallel tracks. Most importantly, the Soviet Union remained China's principal military threat. Moscow still occupied Afghanistan and supported Vietnam. Its military strength continued to increase in the Far East. In the Pacific a growing Soviet fleet threatened vital sea-lanes.

The summit diplomacy of 1984 restored stability and gave some sense of momentum to the Sino-American dialogue, but it did not create the basis of a new relationship. The Reagan-Zhao visits—like normalization—signaled the beginning of a process rather than its culmination.

2

Strategic Triangle: The Impact of Sino-Soviet Relations

Sino-American relations have been shaped by Sino-Soviet relations as well as by relations between the U.S.S.R. and the United States. There has been—and continues to be—a "strategic triangle."

In the 1950s the Chinese Communists' distrust of Washington's policies in the Far East and their perception of the emerging postwar Soviet-American confrontation were the crucial factors that moved Mao and his colleagues to align closely with the Soviet Union. On the other side of the Pacific, it was precisely this close Sino-Soviet relationship that confirmed American suspicions that China was merely another Soviet satellite, an attitude that ultimately contributed to the Sino-American confrontation in Korea.

Toward the end of the 1950s, Sino-Soviet relations began to sour as Soviet Premier Nikita S. Khrushchev promoted a policy of peaceful coexistence with the United States. In Chinese eyes, Moscow appeared to give China's international goals a lower priority than its own policy of détente with Washington. By 1960 Sino-Soviet differences over the proper foreign policy for the socialist camp erupted into the open. As the United States and the

Soviet Union sought coexistence, China set off on its own, seeking an alliance of Third World nations to oppose both superpowers.

For the remainder of Mao's life, the anti-Soviet impulse motivated his American policy. This put the Nixon Administration in the enviable pivotal position in the Sino-Soviet-American triangle as both Moscow and Beijing sought closer relations with the United States.

After Mao's death in 1976 the Soviet Union made a series of high-level overtures to China. The Chinese ignored them. If anything, Mao's successors were even more convinced that the U.S. defeat in Vietnam in 1975 and the steady growth of Soviet influence there had complicated China's security problems. Their concerns seemed justified when Moscow and Hanoi signed a treaty of cooperation and friendship in November 1978. A month later Vietnamese forces invaded Cambodia and overthrew the Pol Pot regime.

In February 1979 China invaded northern Vietnam, but withdrew its troops in less than a month. China wanted to "punish" Vietnam for its tilt toward the Soviet Union without igniting a conflict with Moscow. In March China offered to hold talks with the Soviet Union to resolve mutual problems, and exploratory discussions began that September.

The Soviet invasion of Afghanistan in December led to an immediate worsening of Soviet-American relations and a shift in the politics of the strategic triangle. While Washington became more receptive to the idea of a united front with China against the Soviet Union, Beijing feared that excessive Sino-American hostility toward the Soviet Union might trigger a conflict with the Soviets. Besides, the hardened U.S. approach relieved China of the need to be overly confrontational toward Moscow.

Throughout 1980 Sino-Soviet relations had a curious quality. On the one hand, the sharp polemics continued. Symbolically, China joined the American boycott of the 1980 Olympics in Moscow. On the other, Beijing, anxious to keep its options open, continued informal contacts with the Soviet Union and held talks on river navigation.

In 1981, it was the Soviet Union's turn to exploit the triangular relationship. Aware of Sino-American differences, Moscow flooded Beijing with proposals aimed at improving relations. The Chinese leadership was not receptive until after it had signed the August 1982 agreement with the United States regarding arms sales to Taiwan.

In his September 1982 speech to the 12th Chinese Communist Party Congress in which he unveiled an "independent foreign policy," Hu Yaobang suggested a more open Chinese attitude toward the Soviet Union, but he also underscored three obstacles to normalized relations: Soviet support for Vietnam's invasion of Cambodia, the Soviet occupation of Afghanistan, and the Soviet military presence on the Chinese border.

As Soviet President Leonid I. Brezhnev spoke cryptically of "new things" in China's foreign policy, the first round of Sino-Soviet talks at the vice-foreign ministerial level was about to convene. Although little was accomplished at this first meeting, the warming trend continued. Chinese Foreign Minister Huang Hua attended Brezhnev's funeral, met with his successor Yuri V. Andropov, and left Moscow announcing that he was "optimistic" regarding the course of Sino-Soviet negotiations.

For the next year and a half Sino-Soviet talks continued and relations between the two nations settled into a pattern. The flow of traffic of students, tourists, cultural delegations and sports teams sharply increased. Commercial relations grew, and in 1982 China's trade with the Soviet Union amounted to $307 million.

No progress, however, was made on removing the three obstacles. China failed to drive a wedge between Moscow and Hanoi, Vietnam's capital: the Soviet Union adamantly refused to be drawn into talks affecting "third parties," that is, Vietnam. The U.S.S.R. continued its buildup in the Pacific. Five hundred thousand Soviet troops, supported by increasing numbers of advanced aircraft and nuclear missiles, remained poised along the Chinese border. More ominous still, the Soviet Union increased the number of SS-20 intercontinental ballistic missiles deployed on its Asian front.

Despite slow progress, the Chinese strived to maintain the momentum of better relations with Moscow, and in early 1984 their efforts were rewarded. They signed an agreement with the Soviet Union calling for over $1 billion in trade. When Andropov died in February, the Chinese sent Vice Premier Wan Li, the highest-ranking Chinese official to travel to the Soviet Union in 20 years. At about the same time the forthcoming visit to Beijing of Ivan Arkhipov, Soviet vice-premier, was confirmed. He would be the highest-ranking Soviet to come to China since 1969. On the eve of President Reagan's 1984 visit, it appeared Beijing had succeeded in decoupling Sino-Soviet relations from the Sino-Soviet-American triangle.

This was not the case, however. In April fighting erupted once again on the Sino-Vietnamese border. The Soviet Union supported Vietnam and they held joint amphibious exercises. On May 9 it was announced that the Arkhipov visit would be postponed for "some time." The Soviets were apparently showing their displeasure at the Reagan visit (this despite Chinese censorship of the President's anti-Soviet remarks) as well as solidarity with their Vietnamese allies.

During the summer of 1984 Sino-Soviet invective reached a level of stridency unmatched for two years. In contrast with past crises, Beijing made the first concession. Communist party leader Hu Yaobang told a group of Italian Communist correspondents in September that China had privately informed the Soviets that Beijing would not enter "into any alliance with the United States against the U.S.S.R. Never." This extraordinary statement initially did little to allay Soviet suspicions. As Hu put it, the two nations still did not have "much of a shared language on international issues." But China persevered, setting aside major differences and pursuing those areas where some progress might be possible, namely in the economic realm.

The Chinese press carried features on Soviet reform efforts and growth. It spoke of the complementary nature of the Soviet and Chinese economies: the Soviet Union exported heavy industry, China exported food, light industrial goods and textiles which "precisely met the needs of the Soviet Union." Noting that Moscow could assist it in refurbishing aging Soviet-built factories, China made clear that its "open door" was applicable to the

Soviet Union and Eastern Europe as well as to Western countries.

Vice Premier Arkhipov arrived in China in December for his delayed visit. He had been the head of the Soviet advisers' group in China during the 1950s, and during his talks he recalled those earlier, more halcyon days of Sino-Soviet relations. Arkhipov would discuss only economic questions, Chinese officials later revealed.

Three agreements were signed to further cooperation in economics, trade, and science and technology. The trade goal for 1985 set a month before was revised upward by 22 percent. Both sides expressed the hope that these agreements could form the basis of an improvement in other aspects of the relationship.

Following the death of Soviet President Konstantin U. Chernenko in March 1985 and the accession of Mikhail S. Gorbachev to the post of general-secretary, the two countries made progress on the political front as well. The Chinese sent Vice Premier Li Peng to the funeral with a message from Chinese party leader Hu Yaobang. Li is a strong candidate to succeed Premier Zhao. He is a professional engineer who did graduate work in the Soviet Union during the 1950s.

Hu's message, the first party-to-party communication since the 1960s, broke with precedent. Hu referred to the Soviet Union as a country building "socialism," thus abandoning the Maoist position that the Soviet Union had restored capitalism. On the more personal level, the Chinese press portrayed the new Soviet leader as an energetic reform leader.

Gorbachev was also showing a more open attitude. In his first speech after taking power he stated his desire to "seriously improve" Sino-Soviet relations. In a somewhat unusual move, the Soviets publicized the fact that the Politburo had discussed economic relations with China. In April 1985, Gorbachev mentioned China in the context of the need to promote cooperation among socialist countries.

For the remainder of 1985, these promising signs were substantiated by growing trade and cultural ties. In July, Chinese Vice Premier Yao Yilin arrived in Moscow to sign a five-year,

$14 billion trade agreement which also provided for Soviet assistance in modernizing 17 Chinese industrial enterprises and building 7 new ones. Trade with the Soviet Union in 1985 grew almost 60 percent over 1984, reaching $1.9 billion, according to official Chinese figures. These improved trade relations were probably a major cause of the new Sino-Soviet consular treaty initialed in November. Meanwhile, the exchange of Sino-Soviet cultural delegations also increased at a rapid rate.

However, things did not move as smoothly in the diplomatic realm. To be sure, contacts between officials of both nations increased. Besides the July visit by Yao, there were meetings between Chinese and Soviet foreign ministers in New York as well as Li Peng's December stopover visit with Gorbachev in Moscow as he returned to China from Europe. Finally, the seventh round of Sino-Soviet talks was held in October 1985. Although the future exchange of foreign ministers—no date was set—was agreed upon, the Chinese report of the meeting was gloomy, commenting that there was no resolution of any of the "major conflicts."

Indeed, by the end of 1985 Chinese patience seemed to be wearing thin. Chinese statements suggested a growing suspicion that the Soviets were trying to "dodge" the three obstacles. The new year began with sharp attacks on Soviet policies in Afghanistan and Vietnam and renewed affirmations of China's "independent" foreign policy. At a time when U.S.-Soviet relations seemed to be improving, the impact of the strategic triangle was once more in evidence.

Implications for U.S. Policy

China's relations with the Soviet Union, though dramatically improved since 1982, remain much chillier than Sino-Soviet ties in the 1950s and nowhere near as cordial as Sino-American relations. The next few years will determine whether the warming pattern will continue.

How should the United States react to this thaw in Sino-Soviet relations? Triangular relations, like the weather, are somewhat easier to describe than to do anything about. The United States no longer sees itself pitted against a close Sino-Soviet alliance as it did in the 1950s. It is not being courted by both the Soviet Union and China, as it was in the 1970s, nor is it likely to be again in the near future. Although not entirely comfortable with rapprochement between Washington and Moscow, Beijing does not feel threatened by Soviet-American colloquies, as it did in the late 1960s. Indeed, as its own relations with the Soviet Union improve, China will feel more secure.

If this analysis is correct, U.S.-Chinese relations will evolve within the context of improved Sino-Soviet and Soviet-American relations—a scenario new to the strategic triangle but not necessarily bad for U.S. interests. Improved relations on all sides could give the United States greater latitude both in mending fences with the Soviet Union without arousing Chinese suspicions and improving relations with China without alarming the Soviet Union. The United States should keep its dealings with the Soviet Union and China on separate tracks and not attempt to use bilateral policy to influence the third country.

If China no longer felt immediately threatened by its neighbor and felt secure enough that it could take a genuinely equidistant position between the United States and the Soviet Union, a major element would be removed from the Sino-American relationship and a new basis of the relationship would have to be laid. Whether this happens will be determined in part by the state of Sino-Soviet relations and the development of China's domestic politics; the United States can have little influence over either. But the United States can make a difference in the transition of Sino-American relations to a new and stronger basis.

3

The Taiwan Issue

Of all the problems that stand in the way of improved Sino-American relations, only one is so volatile that it could cause an immediate and grave threat to the ties so carefully nurtured since 1972. This issue is the status of Taiwan.

For the leaders of the People's Republic of China, the continued existence of a Kuomintang regime on Taiwan is a diminution of the Communist party's political authority and an affront to the nation's sovereignty. More specifically, it is a reminder of an incomplete civil war and an incomplete national revolution.

The Communists came to power promising the reestablishment of the territorial integrity of China and an end to foreign interference in the nation's domestic affairs. Yet here is an island, rightfully Chinese, which not only stands apart from China, but maintains international political and economic relations as if it were an independent country. To justify its nationalist credentials, the Communist regime must reclaim the province and end its independent foreign policy. It has been frustrated in achieving this goal, and holds the United States responsible.

No President has been willing to pay the political price for abandoning Taiwan in order to improve relations with China. Although the power of the "Taiwan lobby" has steadily diminished since 1949, articulate and important spokesmen for the rights of 19 million people in Taiwan and their "right" to self-determination remain. Congressional passage of the Taiwan Relations Act of 1979 demonstrated the political cost for any President appearing to abandon the former ally. Successive Administrations have also seen their treatment of Taiwan as a test of the credibility of U.S. obligations abroad.

The overall consensus on Taiwan itself is unquestionably against reunification with China. Both Chiang Kai-shek and his son, Chiang Ching-kuo, who succeeded him in 1978, have maintained—at least formally—that they are the legitimate rulers of all China. In their eyes, the civil war with the Communists continues. Like the leadership in Beijing, they feel that Taiwan should be an integral part of China—but a China ruled by the Kuomintang not the Communists.

This view is shared by most of Taiwan's "mainlanders"—some 15 percent of the current population of 19 million—who came to the island in 1949 and thereafter and continue to dominate its politics and the military. The remaining 85 percent are for the most part ethnic Chinese whose ancestors had come to Taiwan over the last 300 years. They consider Taiwan, not the mainland, home and are not burdened by the legacy of recent history. The civil war on the mainland was not their struggle, and the eventual defeat of the Kuomintang and its relocation to Taiwan was a serious setback which subjected them to rule by a minority outside regime.

By and large the Taiwanese share the government's opposition to becoming part of a Communist-dominated regime. In addition to Beijing's ideology and system, their objections are quite practical: at $3,000, Taiwan's annual per capita income is 10 times that of China, and the Taiwanese seem confident that their political power is on the rise. Although Beijing has pledged that Taiwan will be able to keep its political structure and prospering economic system, its promises do not carry much weight.

Managing the Taiwan Issue

Twice since the Shanghai Communiqué—with the normalization accord of 1978 and the agreement on American arms sales to Taiwan in 1982—the United States and China have made some progress on the Taiwan question. Issues that could be agreed upon were agreed upon; those which could not were set aside for the next round of negotiation. Each side asserted its position on questions still at issue, thereby enabling leaders in both countries to say that they stood fast to their principles. At the same time, clearing away areas of agreement exposed each side's less-flexible positions.

The United States now seems willing to see the Taiwan question solved by the two parties involved and would accept any outcome as long as it is not one that is imposed by force. But Washington has reserved its right to maintain a full range of economic and social relations with the island through the unofficial American Institute in Taiwan, located in Taipei. Taiwan's representatives in this country are granted diplomatic immunity. Two-way trade with Taiwan was nearly $20 billion in 1984, almost three times U.S. trade with China. Investment by American corporations such as General Motors and General Electric plays a significant role in the island's economy. Finally, the Administration has suggested that the future termination of U.S. arms sales is linked to eventual peaceful reunification.

This U.S. view is in direct conflict with the Chinese position, namely that the future of Taiwan should be settled internally and that outsiders should not impose conditions. Chinese statements have suggested that there are circumstances—internal strife in Taiwan that might lead to an independence movement, an unreasonable prolongation of the negotiation process, the development of nuclear weapons by Taipei or a leaning toward the Soviet Union by the Kuomintang—that would be likely to bring military action.

Viewed from Beijing, the full range of U.S.-Taiwan relations hardly seems like noninterference. The most objectionable of the U.S. ties are the sale of U.S. arms and the protective umbrella suggested by the Taiwan Relations Act. Although Washington agreed in 1982 to reduce the level of such sales leading to a "final resolution," the rate of such reduction has been unacceptably slow. In June 1985, the Chinese ambassador to the United States noted that at the current rate of such reductions—about $20 million a year—this process could take 38 years (not to mention possible U.S. adjustments for inflation).

While China remains convinced that American support is a crucial inhibitor to Taiwan's willingness to discuss reconciliation, China's leaders in recent years have sought to avoid confrontation over the Taiwan question and have moved from previous talk of "liberation" to stressing the "peaceful resolution" of the problem. One reason for this more conciliatory approach could be that China, at the moment, does not have the military ability to take the island. But a more likely explanation is that China's leaders have placed priority on foreign-supported economic development, and any use of force would hurt China's reputation as a "responsible" member of the world economic community.

American policy has contributed to this shift on China's part by allowing the Taiwan issue to remain dormant. In contrast with its early months, the Administration has recently shown greater care in its public statements on the Taiwan issue. And it has avoided repeating the error of the 1981 Haig visit, that is, publicly tying progress in U.S.-China relations to Chinese concessions on Taiwan.

China in recent years has mounted a propaganda and diplomatic campaign to win over its compatriots on Taiwan. In January 1979 the Chinese stopped shelling the offshore islands of Quemoy and Matsu and announced, somewhat vaguely, that for at least 50 years after reunification the "status quo" on the island would be respected and "reasonable policies and measures" would be pursued in settling the issue. Subsequently Beijing elaborated that Taiwan would be a "special administrative region with full autonomous power in its internal affairs" and could retain its armed forces; that the "current political and economic system and way of life will remain unchanged" after reunification and that economic relations with foreign countries would be permitted; that political authorities in Taiwan would be given posts in the capital; that individuals from Taiwan would be welcome to travel to the mainland; and that businessmen from Taiwan would be welcome to invest in China.

In the fall of 1984, China used the Sino-British agreement on Hong Kong to demonstrate its commitment to the idea of "one country, two systems." Taiwan, like Hong Kong, could be a capitalist society within a socialist China. In addition, it would retain control over its armed forces. All it had to do was drop its claim to speak for all of China and accept the status of a "special administrative region."

Beijing has tried by every means possible to elicit some response from Taipei. Invitations have been issued to Kuomintang leaders to visit China and regulations have been announced to facilitate travel from Taiwan to the mainland. Ministries in China have been instructed to contact their counterparts in Taiwan and to facilitate trade and investment in China. Fishermen from Taiwan have access to the coastal areas of China, and the Chinese Red Cross has sought to initiate talks similar to those in Korea on the subject of reuniting families. In an attempt to establish a common ground with Taiwan, China's leaders have given prominence to holidays, individuals or organizations that are part of the Nationalist Kuomintang as well as the Communist legacy. All these efforts have brought little response: Taipei continues to stand by its policy of "three no's"— no contact, no talks and no compromises.

View from Taipei

The announcement of full diplomatic relations between the United States and China was a great shock to Taipei. President Chiang Ching-kuo spoke of America's "broken assurances." However, over the past seven years, the island has bounced back from the doldrums. The economy has been doing well, and foreign trade has grown despite Taiwan's diminished international recognition. Although, as Steven I. Levine of American University has argued, political development has not kept pace with economic development, Chiang has expanded the scope of the electoral process and permitted a somewhat circumscribed opposition. On the face of it, there seems to be little incentive to talk with Beijing.

Conservative elements in Taiwan's intelligence and military communities are strongly opposed to any reconciliation with China. Moreover, many of the non-Kuomintang Taiwanese support the regime precisely because they feel it will resist such efforts. Should reunification talks begin, they might withdraw that support or even provide support for an independence movement. They prefer the status quo: neither independence nor reunification. Taiwan also senses some outside pressure against negotiations on reunification. The initiation of such talks could undermine international business confidence in the island and its economy.

Despite these constraints, the regime in Taiwan has permitted direct and indirect contacts with the People's Republic. Delegates from China and Taiwan have attended international meetings together, and their students seem to mix freely in American universities. Both sides had teams at the 1984 Olympics in Los Angeles, with Taiwan identified as "Chinese Taipei" and marching under the Olympic banner rather than its own flag. Finally, there have been reports of business people from Taiwan going to China. In early 1985, Taipei acknowledged two-way trade of nearly half a billion dollars (unofficial estimates put it at twice that). The trade goes through third countries, and the Taiwan government announced in May 1985 that it would not prohibit such indirect trade. Slowly and cautiously economic ties are developing.

The Unresolved Taiwan Question

The Chinese leadership for the time being is taking a patient, restrained approach to resolution of the Taiwan question. Huan Xiang, a leading Chinese commentator on international affairs, spoke last year of giving 20 or 30 years to the negotiation process. He appears to recognize the fact that to coerce Taiwan could have serious consequences for China. It would damage its post-Cultural Revolution international image, call into question its pledge to show restraint in dealing with Hong Kong, and grievously impair relations with its two most important sources of capital and technology: the United States and Japan.

Still, it must be emphasized that the Taiwan question in Sino-American relations, while contained, has not been resolved. During his summer 1985 visit, President Li Xiannian pressed President Reagan on the arms issue and unsuccessfully sought American support for Chinese policy. In October, on the eve of Vice President George Bush's visit to China, the authoritative *Beijing Review* sharply attacked American policy and suggested that Washington was encouraging Taipei's refusal to talk, thus "in effect obstructing the reunification of China." Bush himself received a stern lecture on the subject from his Chinese hosts. American policymakers were thus reminded that they ignore the volatility of this issue at their peril. It remains, to use the words of the article, a "latent crisis."

4

Economic Relations

A century ago New England traders dreamed of the riches to be made in the China market. More recently, an American cosmetics manufacturer looked forward to selling deodorant for "two billion armpits." A century of war, revolution, trade embargoes, and an anticapitalist government in Beijing had apparently not tarnished the glitter of the China trade. At the time of the normalization of relations, it was still perceived by many as a pot of gold just waiting for those clever American business people to find the precise end of the rainbow.

In the years since normalization, the China market has been opened up to Americans to a degree unprecedented in the postwar era. As yet few have found any pots of gold. Rather, American business has finally come up against the realities of trading with China. There has been considerable frustration, but also greater realism.

China's Great Leap Outward

In the wake of the Cultural Revolution, China's reform-minded leadership concluded that they could make up for lost

31

time and rapidly modernize the nation's economy only if foreign trade and investment were made an integral part of economic growth strategy.

The cumulative result of this decision has been the reversal of Mao's policy of "self-reliance" for China in world affairs. The new leadership has sent students abroad to study, shopped for loans in foreign-capital markets, permitted foreign investment under preferential terms and sought Westerners to exploit China's natural resources. To attract business and investors, China has drafted tax laws for foreigners, passed laws on joint ventures and contracts with foreigners, set up courts to settle trade disputes, enacted a patent law, established foreign investment zones (special economic zones), and provided special incentives for foreign investment in certain of the nation's major coastal cities. The foreign presence in China has become almost inescapable.

The impact of these policies on the economic structure of China has been dramatic as new institutions have proliferated and old ones have undergone reform to accommodate the foreign presence. The deeply entrenched Soviet-style planning apparatus has been overhauled. In the early days of Sino-American trade, business people were forced to deal with a few large foreign-trade bureaucracies, often far removed from the actual buyer or seller in China. Since then there has been a gradual process of decentralization, and certain localities and cities now have the right to negotiate for foreign investment. Moreover, factories may in certain cases find their own buyers and sellers abroad. The October 1984 reform of the economy, which called for the introduction of price reform, was in part a response to economic pressures from the foreign sector to ensure that foreign technologies would be used most efficiently and that goods sold abroad would be priced in relation to their true cost.

Not since the mid-1950s, when the Chinese adopted the Soviet economic model to make it easier to absorb Soviet assistance, has such a major domestic reform taken place. According to Chinese reports, the overall results have been impressive. During the first six months of 1985, foreign loans and investments were put at $3.1 billion, a sizable increase over the same period in 1984. The

By Meyer for *The San Francisco Chronicle.*

number of joint ventures with foreign investors was said to have grown dramatically. In the first half of 1985, agreements for 687 more were signed, four times the number signed during the first half of 1984.

Foreign trade, which totaled $20 billion in 1978, reached $48 billion in 1984 and, reportedly, $67 billion in 1985. China's major imports are machinery, iron and steel, foodstuffs and textile fibers. Its major exports are manufactured goods, most importantly textiles and clothing, agricultural products and petroleum. Before the 1970s food was China's leading export; it has been overtaken by manufactured goods, with petroleum occupying an increasingly important place.

These figures make clear that China's trade strategy is to import foreign plants and technology to produce light industrial goods which, along with petroleum and agricultural products, will provide the exports to pay for the foreign machinery and technology. China is, today, one of the world's leading petroleum exporters and, with successful reforms in agriculture, is beginning to compete with the United States in certain Asian grain markets. While exportable surpluses of these two items will decline as Chinese domestic needs increase, they remain staples of its foreign trade.

The direction of trade has also shifted. In 1960 approximately 60 percent of China's trade was with Communist-bloc countries. By 1985, according to figures released by the Ministry of Foreign Economic Relations and Trade, most of China's trade was with non-Communist countries, with Japan ($20.2 billion), Hong Kong ($11.9 billion) and the United States ($7.2 billion) representing nearly 60 percent of total trade. The shift is indicative of China's quest for the best technology currently available.

Economically, as Michel Oksenberg of the University of Michigan has argued, China has "joined the world." China's export-oriented strategy, its growing reliance on foreign lending and its membership in numerous international economic bodies all demonstrate this fact. China finds its economy scrutinized, its exports such as petroleum subject to world market conditions or, in the case of light industry, subject to protectionist impulses, and its freedom of action limited by growing international commitments. The new leadership has sacrificed much of the autonomy and independence that Mao prized so highly.

China has also managed to change radically its image in the international community, witness the reaction to the 1984 agreement with Britain regarding the future status of Hong Kong. China promised that Hong Kong could keep its present "capitalist system and life-style" untouched for 50 years after it reverted to China in 1997. For Beijing to agree beforehand how it would treat a part of China was a considerable concession that represented a sensitivity to international financial concerns and a bid to Taiwan. Equally significant was the fact that most of the international economic community, excluding Taiwan, was willing to accept China's word on the future of Hong Kong. China seemed to have gained considerable international credibility.

Sino-American Relations: The Economic Dimension

How has this changed policy affected China's economic relations with the United States? At the time of normalization there were several "unresolved economic issues" between the United States and China, as Harry Harding Jr. of the Brookings Institution noted in a joint Asia Society/Foreign Policy Association special publication, *China and the U.S.*, written in 1979. One by one, many of these questions were dispensed with. In early 1979 the two governments reached an agreement on the question of assets blocked during the cold-war years. Later that year, China was given access to Export-Import Bank credits. In 1980 the United States relaxed restrictions on technology transfers, and China was granted most-favored-nation status. In subsequent years there were a number of agreements in such areas as airline service, the establishment of consulates, promotion of Sino-American trade, and wheat purchases. Economic links seemed to be binding the two countries together.

In the 1980s American oil companies, including Chevron Corporation and Texaco, began to explore for offshore oil in the South China Sea. With the Reagan Administration's important decision in 1983 to facilitate technology transfers to China, the Chinese finally felt that the hopes they had placed in normalization might be realized.

The United States has helped upgrade China's technology through educational and scientific exchanges. In addition to hundreds of joint research projects between scientists of both nations and the exchange of scientific data and materials, American and Chinese scholars have taught in each other's universities. Most important have been the educational exchanges. In the academic year 1983-84 some 12,000 Chinese students and scholars, mostly in the sciences, were in the United States under government programs, university exchanges or private auspices. One scholar has estimated that American universities have spent nearly $80 million on Chinese exchange students.

The volume and content of trade since normalization reflect these dramatic changes in Sino-American economic relations. In 1978 Sino-American trade stood at $1.2 billion. By 1985, according to recently revised Chinese figures, it stood at $7.2 billion, a 600 percent increase. The content of the trade also changed somewhat. Before 1984 the principal American exports to China were agricultural—grain and textile fibers—with machinery and transport equipment coming next. Chinese exports were heavily concentrated in textiles and clothing (nearly 50 percent) and petroleum products (approximately 20 percent). In 1984, as a result of the loosening of restrictions on technology transfer and China's improved agricultural situation, the "computer and office machinery" component of U.S. sales to China doubled to $101 million. Most analysts saw the rising technology exports as a portent for the future.

There has also been significant growth in American investment in China since normalization. In late 1985 the total value of American investment was put at $700 million. The Shanghai Foxboro Corporation, the joint venture for the manufacture of electrical instruments that President Reagan visited in April 1984, is but one example. U.S. corporations are now a prominent part of the economic landscape in China. Occidental Petroleum Corporation is a partner in a $650 million project to develop China's largest opencut coal mine. American hotel corporations are participating in a number of joint ventures. As Chevron Corporation searches for oil offshore, American Motors Corporation makes Jeeps in Beijing, the American Tobacco Company produces Camel cigarettes, and Coleco Industries Inc. turns out its Cabbage Patch doll bodies. Nabisco Brands Inc. has agreed to produce Ritz crackers in Beijing, and McDonnell Douglas Corporation will manufacture commercial jetliners in Shanghai.

What factors will influence the development of economic relations in the near future? The state of political relations will be crucial. A second factor relates to the economic needs and capabilities of each side. It is clear that American business has a good deal to offer China. The crucial question is: How will China pay for these goods and services? Although it has been granted large credit lines and has strong foreign exchange reserves, China must still consider its export capabilities. Indeed, in 1985 China faced a number of serious issues in its foreign trade sector. In an unusual move, China's General Administration of Customs released figures in January 1986 that suggested a trade deficit of $13.7 billion for 1985. This was nearly twice the figure released by the Ministry of Foreign Economic Relations and Trade.

Moreover, John Stuermer of the First National Bank of Chicago, writing in *The China Business Review*, estimated that China had expended $7 billion in foreign exchange reserves during 1985. By the end of that year, he estimated that China held approximately $12 billion in reserves. Although Stuermer notes that this is not yet a serious situation, the Chinese themselves have expressed concern that China might become another Third World debtor country. By the end of 1985 they were moving to restrict the level of imports. China does not demand balanced bilateral trade, but it does seek to avoid large imbalances. The big question mark in Sino-American trade is the status of the two major exports—textiles and petroleum.

U.S. domestic demands for restrictions on imports of textiles and clothing have been a perennial bone of contention between the United States and China as they have been with virtually all U.S. trading partners. In August 1984 the Reagan Administration announced a change in the rules for the import of textiles: goods semifinished in one country and then shipped to another for final processing before shipment to the United States would be counted against the import quota of the first country. For China, which ships large amounts of semifinished goods to Hong Kong for export to the United States under that colony's more liberal quota, this was a serious economic threat. The Chinese protested that it would constitute a "grievous blow" to the Chinese economy and would cost some 60,000 jobs.

By the fall a small trade war had broken out. At the end of the year it was apparent that China would not fulfill its agreement to purchase 6 million metric tons of American grain. Although this might have been due to China's excellent grain harvest, some saw it as retaliation for the textile import quotas. The battle over protectionism was rekindled in late 1985. The Chinese claimed that a bill passed by Congress to limit textile and clothing imports would reduce China's quota by 56 percent, causing losses of more than $500 million a year in exports to the United States. A crisis was averted when President Reagan vetoed the bill. But the protectionism issue remained.

The situation with regard to petroleum could also become serious. China is said to be second to Saudi Arabia in terms of reserves. Oil exports stood at $5 billion during 1984, and those exports probably grew in 1985. Despite failures, frustrations and uncertainty about the rules of the game, American oil companies and drilling-supply corporations have persevered. The oil companies are driven by the promise of China's reserves, while suppliers covet a major market for sophisticated American exploration and drilling equipment. To date this crucial area of Sino-American cooperation has shown somewhat disappointing results. Moreover, the early 1986 fall in oil prices suggests that China will have to produce substantially more oil to maintain its foreign exchange earnings from this sector; it is not clear this will be feasible.

Another factor influencing the future growth of the Sino-American economic relationship is the foreign-trade and investment institutions that are being established to facilitate economic ties. Tales about the difficulty of dealing with the Chinese bureaucracy are legion. As a result of decentralization, foreigners no longer deal with familiar bureaucracies but must contend with middle-level and even factory-level administrations. Moreover, foreign joint ventures must often search out their own suppliers and buyers; in the past they could rely on state suppliers.

Coping with the American bureaucracy can be equally formidable. In a February 1985 article in *The Wall Street Journal*, former Assistant Secretary of State Richard C. Holbrooke noted that while a routine request for an export license took 29 days, more complicated ones could take an average of 117 days. If the item required approval from the Coordinating Committee (CO-COM), consisting of representatives from all North Atlantic Treaty Organization countries except Iceland, plus Japan, which was established to prevent strategic goods from reaching Communist countries, the waiting period could average an additional 283 days. During his October 1985 visit to China, Vice President Bush informed his Chinese hosts that an agreement had been reached within COCOM to reduce the number of technological items for export to China that would be subject to review. He also announced that the number of licenses granted by the United States had increased to 5,600 through July 1985.

The Chinese nevertheless remain suspicious about U.S. willingness to export technology to their country. In a December interview, China's foreign minister, Wu Xueqian, said that his nation was often treated like a "hidden opponent."

A roadblock that prevented the sale of U.S. nuclear power equipment to China appeared to have been removed by the agreement President Reagan signed on his 1984 trip to that country. The American nuclear power industry began looking forward to as much as $10 billion in sales and the creation of 50,000 American jobs. However, the agreement ran into problems almost immediately after the President's return. Some congressmen suspected that the Chinese were helping Pakistan develop nuclear weapons; others were concerned about the lack of control over spent fuel. During his July 1985 visit to the United States, President Li Xiannian clarified the Chinese position and the agreement was signed. However, although Congress approved the agreement in December, it did so in an atmosphere of distrust regarding Chinese statements on nuclear proliferation that angered the Chinese.

On the Chinese side, attempts to revamp their foreign trade structure and improve its efficiency have increased the woes of foreign business people. The reform movement is proceeding on a trial and error basis, subject to the shifting currents of Chinese politics. Rules are literally being made as the system moves along, and subsequent clarifications or policy reversals can change the basis of earlier agreements. Before American business invests heavily, regulations regarding taxation, technology licensing, sales within China and profit repatriation will have to be clarified. Moreover, in 1978-79 and again in 1980-81 and 1985 the Chinese increased foreign imports dramatically, only to cut them back abruptly to right the balance of payments. Foreign business is thus very vulnerable to the ebb and flow of economic reform in China.

American business remains cautiously optimistic about the China market and the opportunities to solve some of the major bottlenecks in the Chinese economy—communications, electronics, energy development and food processing, among others. The optimism is based on the assumption that the current reform movement will continue and that over time some of the institutional obstacles will be eliminated. There is a general belief that a leadership committed to raising the standard of living, upgrading the technological level of its industry and promoting market-oriented economic reforms is a very promising future business partner.

中國

5

China's Reform Process

Deng Xiaoping has likened China's reform effort to that of a "second revolution." He is hardly exaggerating. Deng's program is extraordinarily ambitious and complex, and it is being closely watched by the outside world. He has tried to assure foreign visitors that they could "rely on the continuity" of China's reform, but concedes they are "not thoroughly convinced."

As Robert Dernberger, professor of economics at the University of Michigan, has argued, in the years since Chairman Mao's death the Chinese leadership has not only tackled the legacy of his radical vision; it has also taken on the task of reforming the policies and institutions of the Soviet-style economy which he established during the mid-1950s.

The issue of the Maoist legacy was tackled almost immediately, at first somewhat tentatively by Hua Guofeng, who came to power after Mao's death, and then more aggressively by Deng. The major Maoist tenet to be revised was that of continual revolution. Soon after his death, Mao's successors announced that the major class struggles had ended in China; economic construction would take precedence. They also abandoned Mao's strictures regarding self-reliance. China's involvement in the world economy became an integral feature of its development model. In industry and agriculture, they emphasized material incentives, which had been discouraged during the Cultural Revolution. In the urban areas, the regime announced wage increases and bonuses. In the rural areas, although the collective farm structure remained intact until 1980-81, the government raised procurement prices, restored private plots and reopened local markets. Finally, the leaders turned to the intellectuals, earlier excoriated for their bourgeois tendencies, to help modernize the nation. To assure a continuous stream of talent, they reinstituted the pre-Cultural Revolution emphasis on quality in China's educational system.

Deng consolidated his control over the Maoists and the Maoist legacy at the June 1981 meeting of the party's Central Committee. Mao's direct responsibility for the horrors of the Cultural Revolution was finally acknowledged. At the same time it was announced that Deng's protégé, Hu Yaobang, would replace Mao's hand-picked successor, Hua Guofeng, as the head of the party. Hua had already relinquished the premiership to another Deng protégé, Zhao Ziyang, the previous year.

Deng's victory over the Maoists at the upper levels of the party was complete, but many who had gained influence during the Cultural Revolution remained in the middle and lower ranks of certain bureaucracies. Indeed, almost half of the party's 40 million members joined during those years. The military, too, appeared to have serious reservations about the course of post-Mao China. The issue of political support remained unresolved as Deng confronted the second major legacy of the Communist party of China—the Soviet model.

The Stalinist approach to economic development places the government in control of the entire economy. The state or the collective not only owns the major means of production, but the planners set the priorities for the society which powerful ministries in charge of the individual enterprises then carry out. Factory managers, who are expected to achieve quantitative

Photo by Sheila Phalon.
Proprietor of a free-enterprise fish stand.

targets, are held on extremely tight rein by centralized ministries. Prices are set by the planners and do not reflect supply and demand.

The result is a society where the lack of freedom in the economy is paralleled by its absence in the political realm. Policy reflects the preferences of the political leadership; it is not the product of bargaining and compromise between the leaders and various social groups. As one specialist has argued, the government in a Leninist-Stalinist system is not so much a gyroscope, adjusting to the desires of society, as it is a motor driving society.

In describing their approach to this reform, the Chinese speak of the need to "enliven" the economy. In general what this means is that Deng and his allies are trying to loosen the administrative constraints on the economic system while providing the incentives for individual actors—be they farmers, workers or factory managers—to increase productivity. The result has been the dismantling of some of the institutional structure of Stalinism, a new emphasis on increasing living standards as a goal of socialism, and the unleashing of considerable entrepreneurial energy in the economy as a whole.

Economic Reform

China is overwhelmingly rural, so it is perhaps fitting that the reform began in the countryside in 1979 when the Chinese cautiously introduced the "responsibility system." By 1986 it was in effect in practically all of rural China. Under the responsibility system, the collective assigns portions of land to households in return for an agreed fee. The family is expected to sell a contracted amount of production to the state. All production beyond this can be disposed of by the families on the open market. In addition, "specialized households" are encouraged to engage in activities that range from fish raising to flower production to running restaurants to pooling resources with other families to opening small factories. In 1984 it was announced that tenancy contracts could be for as long as 15 years and could be transferred to other families. Within five years the Chinese had dismantled collectivized agriculture.

The results of higher crop prices and this unleashing of peasant entrepreneurship in the Chinese countryside have been dramatic. From 1953 to 1978 agricultural output grew at an average rate of 3.2 percent per year. In the years 1979-83 average annual growth was between 7 and 8 percent. In one area of China in that period, rural income grew from 135 yuan (about $47) to 310 yuan (about $109). Signs of prosperity—new houses, television sets, refrigerators, etc.—in the countryside have been a common theme in the Chinese press.

However, the benefits of reform have by no means been equally shared. Some areas have done better than others. Forty percent of China's countryside is still without electricity. In October 1984, Hu Yaobang spoke of the need to solve "the problem of food and clothing for 60 million people in the rural areas." The uneven distribution of the economic benefits of reform has been one of the hallmarks—and vulnerabilities—of the reform movement.

To make the centrally planned economy more efficient and, most importantly, to assure the most effective use of Western technology, China made two further landmark decisions in 1984. In April, the government extended to 14 coastal cities and the island of Hainan investment incentives under terms similar to those in the special economic zones established five years earlier. Western businesses could now move directly into some of the cities (such as Canton and Shanghai) which before 1949 had been the recipients of considerable foreign investment—and control— and which were among the best endowed in China in terms of transportation facilities and labor force.

This decision was followed in October 1984 by a sweeping reform of the industrial economy. Obligatory planning, except for a few major items, was to be replaced by guidance planning. In regard to enterprise management, the state would relax its control over most firms and allow them to arrange for their own raw materials, seek customers, manage profits after the payment of a tax to the state, and set the terms of wages for the workers. Finally, and most importantly, the government announced that many prices would be adjusted to respond—at least in important part—to market forces.

The reforms being proposed are bold in conception. However, much of the program is yet to be widely implemented. Moreover, it must be emphasized that the economy as a whole is very far from being capitalist. Although some citizens are permitted to form small companies or service organizations, the major productive forces of the society are still owned by the state. In agriculture, although a system of contracting with the peasantry has replaced the earlier method of state procurement, the state can still use its economic power to exert enormous influence. In industry, the planning structure remains in place, most prices are still set by the state and the state maintains considerable control over the funds and raw materials available to the various enterprises. The system is no more capitalist than Western economies with strong government intervention are socialist or Communist.

Neither is China a democracy. China is still very much a society directed from the top. Deng has been much more open to "liveliness" in the economic realm than in the political realm.

Despite some increased political stability and greater openness in the cultural field, the atmosphere for creative intellectuals in China remains akin to what it had been in the past: pledges of great creative freedom are followed by warnings regarding excessive "liberalism."

The political reforms are quite modest in scope. They largely seek to assure that those favorable to Deng's reforms occupy key positions to make the administered society work better. At top levels of the party, Deng has attempted to achieve what eluded Mao—the establishment of a succession process. Deng is 81. Over the past few years he has yielded considerable power to two individuals, Zhao Ziyang, 66, the premier of China, and Hu Yaobang, 70, the party general-secretary. They are obviously not young men. Very recently there has been evidence that a still younger generation of top leaders is emerging. It includes a 56-year-old party bureaucrat, Hu Qili, Li Peng, 57, and Tian Jiyun, 56, both vice-premiers, and Qiao Shi, 60, a party administrator. All these men along with Vice Premier Yao Yilin and Foreign Minister Wu Xueqian were elected to the Politburo in September 1985. When Vice Premier Li Peng accompanied Chinese President Li Xiannian to the United States in July 1985, he was given very special attention because, as one U.S. official put it, "He's a possible future premier." Others among this group have similarly traveled abroad and have been given greater political responsibilities.

At the middle and lower levels, the problems are formidable. Many in the party occupying middle-level positions were recruited before 1956 and have few of the skills necessary to cope with the new policies. One survey showed that only 18 percent of the party's members had a college or senior middle-school education. Moreover, their image of socialist China must differ considerably from Deng's. One of the significant developments in the 1983-84 "antispiritual pollution" campaign, which was intended to crack down on "unhealthy" tendencies such as vulgar dress and Western rock music, was the fact that many in the lower levels of the party eagerly used the campaign to oppose the reform movement.

Over the past few years, Deng and his colleagues have sought to deal with these problems by conducting a campaign within the party to encourage mandatory retirement and to recruit technically trained individuals. As of 1986, this campaign was beginning to show some results with as many as 1 million cadres reportedly replaced at lower levels.

One might argue that movement toward capitalism and democracy may occur as Western ideas filter into China or intellectuals call for political democratization. Such an outcome of the reform is possible, but other outcomes seem more likely. What are these outcomes and what implications do they have for Sino-American relations?

The Results of Reform

Deng has sought to achieve virtually a second revolution in China by boldly and bluntly confronting major problems in the economy and polity. He has accomplished a great deal. He has changed the political and ideological tone that prevailed in China at the death of Mao. The economy has been invigorated. Agricultural production is up, the West is participating in the nation's economy, and the industrial system has begun to show signs of throwing off the shackles of the old centrally administered system. Deng's frequent claim that the best guarantee for the continuation of the reforms lies in their mass popularity seems to be substantiated by the dramatic changes that have occurred in the nation's standard of living. In the decade since the death of Mao, Deng and his colleagues have achieved a transformation of China that few would have thought possible in 1976.

Yet having said this, one must also note some of the vulnerabilities of the reform effort. In their enthusiasm for the recent policies in China, many commentators have not taken sufficient note of the reforms' limitations and problems. The very boldness and speed of these changes have generated numerous problems that might ultimately undermine the effort. To avoid a repetition of Chinese realities smashing romanticized American views of China, these problems must be addressed and understood.

In agriculture, even the immensely successful responsibility system has not been without problems. Since agriculture is still overwhelmingly labor intensive, the responsibility system encourages large families and so undercuts the "one-child family" campaign. There is evidence that less attention is being paid in the countryside to such collective concerns as health and welfare. The number of those engaged in farming has been declining as more peasants turn to commercial activities. The responsibility system has also created a certain amount of social tension as differences between richer and poorer peasants have become more obvious. Political decay is also evident. Formerly powerful rural party bureaucrats now find themselves with less influence as the importance of collective structures declines. Many are seeking to cash in on the prosperity by using their political connections to secure economic gain.

Perhaps the greatest matter for concern is the fact that much of the newly acquired peasant income is going into consumption rather than investment. Indeed, although the government has indirectly put more money into agriculture through raising the price paid the farmers for their produce, there has been very little direct state investment in such areas as fertilizers and mechanization. Many Western economists argue that the recent gains in agricultural production are the result of organizational change and will not be sustained unless the state is willing to invest more heavily.

Although the industrial reform is still at a very early stage, problems ranging from poor coordination and confusion to mismanagement to corruption are emerging. The large foreign trade deficit incurred by China during 1985 has already been noted. This was symptomatic of an economy that was showing signs of overheating due, in part, to the weakness of central administrative control. The center was finding it difficult to maintain control not only over provincial foreign trade but also over capital expenditures by local authorities. Although they would have preferred to use more-indirect fiscal methods of controlling the economy, the central authorities in China were forced in 1985 to revert to older administrative methods in an attempt to achieve overall economic control. China's leaders have

Photo by Sheila Phalon.

Building a hotel to accommodate tourism boom.

yet to find a way to achieve a controlled "enlivening" of the national economy.

At the factory level there are also problems. Many managers find it difficult to obtain the raw materials and machinery that used to be supplied by the state. New freedoms are also being used irresponsibly. For example, the Bank of China during late 1984 issued large numbers of loans, raising the money supply to potentially inflationary levels. Pent-up worker unhappiness with wage levels led to the indiscriminate granting of bonuses, which seemed to bear little relation to productivity. Rising wage funds added to the danger of inflation.

Local industrial managers are using the difficulty of obtaining materials and the freedom to set sales prices as a way of reaping great profits through price gouging. Recently news came from China of an office that sold the same shipment of automobiles several times over at great profit. Corruption is finding its way into the administrative apparatus of the party and the state.

Cadres seem to be cashing in on the confusion generated by the changes in the planning system by using their political influence to obtain goods and services. As one Chinese newspaper reported, the attitude seems to be, "A piece of information means a handful of money." By summer 1985, the regime found it necessary to decree that party and state offices would not be allowed to engage in business, and for the rest of the year official corruption was a major issue.

Changes in the price structure have created additional confusion, and the impact on the urban worker has been profound. Since most foods, housing and consumer goods are highly subsidized by the state, the introduction of more market-oriented prices has meant an increase in the cost of living for most of China's workers. In some cases the state is cushioning the increase by cost-of-living adjustments. But the danger of a lower standard of living or inflation remains, and China has called a halt to price reform during 1986. Ironically, urbanites, who still enjoy a higher standard of living than those in the rural areas, seem to be showing their insecurity by looking with envy upon the peasants who, they feel, are getting ahead under the new reforms.

By the fall of 1985, all these problems with the economic reform had become apparent. Indeed, at a September party meeting Chen Yun, one of China's senior leaders and a politician with broad economic experience, used the occasion to air his concerns. Peasant flight from agriculture to commercial enterprises, he argued, endangered the nation's ability to feed itself. Although he affirmed his support for the reforms, Chen criticized the new emphasis on market forces and called for greater planning and central control of the economy. Finally, his sharpest barbs were reserved for those party members who had "forsaken the socialist and Communist ideals" in search of monetary gain. He singled out those who turned their backs on "national dignity" in dealing with foreigners.

Chen's words could not be ignored. He was not only a widely respected leader, he had also hit on some major problems with the reform. During the remainder of 1985, there was evidence of retrenchment by Deng and his colleagues. There was a very harsh

Photo by Sheila Phalon.
The number of automobiles has increased, but pedal-power is still important.

assault on official corruption. There was some crackdown on what Chen had called "capitalist" ideological tendencies. The special economic zones received a hard second look. The release of China's Seventh Five-Year Plan (1986-1990) affirmed the thrust of the reform movement, but reflected much of Chen's insistence on a slower growth rate and greater control. Indeed, as of January 1986, it seemed that China was trying to digest some of the reforms of the past seven years and deal with some of the acknowledged problems while continuing to affirm the direction of reforms.

The Future of Reform

The events of late 1985 point up the strengths and also the weaknesses of the reform group in China. The reformers, and particularly Deng, have displayed considerable political skill and acumen. They have made masterful use of the maxim that "nothing succeeds like success": they have used higher agricultural production and the improved standard of living as evidence of the correctness of their program. In addition, when they have run into problems, they have dealt forcefully with them even while appearing to make concessions to their opponents.

The key to this strategy has been the presence of Deng who, by the force of his personality and pervasive influence in the political system, has been able to maintain the momentum of reform. China is still a very personalistic political system.

Most analysts of Chinese politics feel that the chances for the successful continuation of the reform effort will be increased if Deng remains politically active during the next five years. However, should Deng die or become incapacitated during the present formative and still uncertain stage of the reform movement, parts of the post-Mao reform program could be reversed.

The list of potential opponents of the reform process is formidable: members of the economic bureaucracy who will lose their positions; the military who continue to receive a declining share of the rapidly growing state budget and whose numbers are being reduced through demobilization; ideological and public-security bureaucrats who are fretting over the consequences of greater economic autonomy and a larger foreign presence; and ill-trained or suspect cadres who might face early retirement.

At the top, should they survive Deng, two figures would undoubtedly play key roles. They are Chen Yun and Peng Zhen, both in their early eighties. Both have expressed their concerns about the scope of the reform movement. Chen's recent statements about freedom in the economy, ideological discipline and the extent of the opening toward the West have already been noted. It should be added that, according to some reports, he has favored a more distant policy vis-à-vis the United States, and his warm greeting of his old friend Vice Premier Arkhipov did not go unnoticed in the West. Peng Zhen, a former mayor of Beijing and an early victim of the Cultural Revolution, seems to be more concerned with law and order. Peng and Chen represent an important school of thought in China that seems to feel that the opening to the West has gone too far and that more discipline and planning are needed in society. Should either or both of these men succeed to the shadowy role of "paramount leader" or should problems with the reform movement increase their influence, a very different China might emerge. Even if these individuals do not assume the leadership, the coalition that might form around them appears to be the principal political alternative to the Deng reform movement.

Such a grouping would probably not change two fundamental policies of Deng. The first is the rejection of the radical, socialist vision of Mao, and the second is the commitment to an "independent foreign policy." The call for independence and global nonalignment resonates strongly with China's historical concerns with loss of initiative and victimization in global politics.

However, one could imagine this concern with national independence fueling limits on China's openness to foreign trade, investment and culture. In addition, such an opposition coalition might call for a renewal of central economic controls and the imposition of tighter reins on social change. With such a coalition in charge, China might attenuate economic ties with the United States and, if relations with the Soviet Union improved, would likely seek more-distant strategic ties with Washington.

Finally, a worst-case scenario would see domestic conflict leading to victory by no coalition. Rather political stalemate might lead to broad social unrest, breakdown in the economy, political instability and an uncertain foreign policy.

However, for the moment, the momentum seems to be with the reformers. Although they have momentarily slowed the process of reform, the commitment to change has not waned. There is reason to be cautiously optimistic that the reforms will continue. Still, the possibility that a less reform-oriented coalition might emerge is also real. It cannot be dismissed as we ponder the future of China.

美國

6

The Future of the Relationship

Are China and the United States developing the kind of mutual understanding that is the basis of a continuing relationship? One cannot easily answer such a question. Many American students who have spent time in China are more sensitive to the cultural nuances of China, but how many have returned home frustrated by the difficulties of work and research in China? How many business people have abandoned the China market, thwarted by its cumbersome methods and bureaucracy? And how many tourists return home mistaking street peddlers and foreign-made television sets for "capitalism"?

Many Chinese have as unrealistic a picture of the United States as Americans have of China. The expression that for some the "moon is rounder" in the West encapsulates this tendency to idealize the West. Other Chinese have, like their American counterparts, returned home with negative feelings engendered by poverty and anti-Asian sentiments in the United States. Many Chinese remain ambivalent about their country's relations with the West in general and the United States in particular.

If strong and consistent relations are to develop, much work remains to be done. This is a most difficult but also a most important item on the agenda as China and the United States enter the second decade after normalization.

The Domestic Political Dimension

Whether it was Wisconsin Senator Joseph McCarthy's Communist witch-hunt in the United States or the frenzy of the Cultural Revolution in China, domestic politics have played an important role in Sino-American relations. They are likely to continue to do so in the future. On the American side, while there seems to be considerable bipartisan support for the growing relationship with China, this could change. If China remains on its current reform course, there is every reason to expect sharpening Sino-American differences over economic issues. In addition, any Chinese attempt to resolve the Taiwan question by force would bring a sharp backlash in the United States. While it is not certain that any future Administration would actually defend Taiwan, an attack would almost certainly destroy the prevailing consensus in favor of close ties with China. It is perhaps useful to recall that the current becalmed state of the China issue in American politics is the historical exception, not the rule.

Beyond being prepared for the unpredictable in Chinese politics, is there anything American policymakers can or should do regarding domestic political developments in China? The simple answer is, very little. On the other hand, if the United States does not handle the important issues on the Sino-American agenda correctly, relations could be damaged or the position of those within China who seek to derail the reform effort could be strengthened.

The Taiwan Dimension

While neither side at present seeks a test of wills over Taiwan, both will have relatively little room to maneuver when future questions regarding the island arise.

One such question relates to arms sales. Even as the United States edges toward arms sales to China, Taiwan's supporters in the United States press for assistance in modernizing the island's defenses. A difficult choice may soon face the Administration: to assist in the modernization of Taiwan's military and possibly upset relations with China, or solidify Sino-American ties by selling arms to Beijing and spark a demand for equal treatment for Taiwan.

Developments within Taiwan can affect America's choice. The crucial political issue on Taiwan is the succession to the office of president. Economically, there are also potential problems. Although the economy has shown strong growth, the financial system of the island is considered antiquated and was rocked in 1985 by a large bank scandal. Moreover, Taiwan's economy is oriented toward export growth. This has made the island's prosperity more vulnerable to foreign business cycles and protectionist sentiments. For all these reasons, some predict a rocky period ahead for Taiwan's economy.

Should a more intransigent leadership group or, though unlikely, a Taiwan independence candidate succeed President Chiang, China might feel compelled to put military pressure on the island. Similarly, should there be an economic or political breakdown, Chinese leaders have made it clear they would intervene to restore order—and take control.

Even in the absence of such changes in Taiwan, there are circumstances that might cause Chinese leaders to end the present relatively moderate policy. An American policy reversal or changed perceptions in China could prompt Beijing to pressure the United States to further distance itself from Taiwan. Or new leadership in China could decide to resort to coercion to resolve the issue.

While Americans would prefer a continuation of the present slow process of reconciliation, the other two possibilities cannot be ruled out. They would put Washington into a very difficult position of choosing between China and Taiwan.

The Strategic Dimension

In the strategic area, the task for American policymakers is to explore those issues of international politics on which they can secure some consensus with the Chinese. The basis for the future relationship could be the two countries' common interests in the

Pacific region. The still significant Soviet threat to China could be considered within the broader context of shared interests with the United States in such areas as Southeast Asia and the Korean peninsula. Such an approach would draw in other American allies in the region, particularly Japan, and give China a greater opportunity to play a constructive role as a Pacific power.

Sino-American interests converge on coping with Soviet military power and political influence in Asia. Examples of that growing influence include the Soviet-Vietnamese entente, Indian Prime Minister Rajiv Gandhi's 1985 trip to the Soviet Union, the increasing North Korean tilt toward Moscow, and finally Gorbachev's resurrection in early 1985 of a Soviet collective security proposal for Asia. Soviet efforts in the region are likely to increase.

Other issues on which Sino-American interests coincide in Asia include the Japanese-American security relationship, maintaining peace on the Korean peninsula, opposing the Vietnamese invasion of Cambodia, supporting Thailand and backing ASEAN (the Association of Southeast Asian Nations). Farther West, China backs Pakistan, an American ally in the region. Obviously, there is much ground for the development of a strategic vision based on common interests in the area.

Placing Sino-American relations more firmly within such a regional context would have other advantages. Even if it does not assure policy coordination with U.S. friends in Asia, at least their reactions will be considered. The United States, for example, has not always taken into account Japan's interests in formulating its China policy. Moreover, the United States sometimes has forgotten that many Southeast Asian nations view the prospect of an economically and militarily powerful China with foreboding and see American policy toward China as creating a potential regional threat. Placing China's development within a regional context might lessen their distrust.

This will not be an easy task: there is no historical precedent for regional cooperation between a strong China, Japan and the United States. Moreover, amidst the common interests lies the potential for discord: Japan and the United States are potential competitors for economic influence in China and in the region as a whole. A North Korean shift toward Moscow might compel China to play a role in Korea that is less supportive of Japanese-American interests. China's support for New Zealand's opposition to the visit of nuclear-armed warships suggests that China is capable of interfering in America's relations with its Pacific allies. This is an ominous sign given China's on-again, off-again support of Japan's security relationship with the United States. Finally, differences with China could develop over American moves to improve relations with Vietnam and Chinese support for the Khmer Rouge, who were overthrown when North Vietnam invaded Cambodia.

However, should the United States and China succeed in developing a strategic vision based on common interests in the region, it would unquestionably clarify, if not resolve, another outstanding issue in Sino-American relations—the question of military cooperation and arms sales.

Many American government officials feel that military ties are an important component of the relations between two friendly nations, and there was considerable enthusiasm in Washington as arms sales to China seemed to be reaching fruition. In September the Pentagon submitted to Congress a proposal for selling an ammunition factory to China. In April 1986 it was announced that the United States was selling advanced avionics to China's air force valued at $550 million and was considering sales to China's navy.

However, the United States must consider some of the drawbacks of such sales. These include a possible congressional crisis over arms sales to Taiwan; opposition on the part of China's Asian neighbors; and the danger of provoking Moscow.

The Chinese will be weighing similar factors. U.S. military aid would be costly internationally. It would hurt China's nonaligned image in the Third World, affect ties with the Soviet Union and promote the modernization of the military on Taiwan.

The Chinese must also consider the domestic fallout of a military relationship with the United States. Although Deng might want to give new weapons to the service branches that have supported him, the funds for arms purchases are in short supply. The U.S. government has estimated that the cost of modernizing the Chinese military would be nearly the equivalent of the entire Chinese budget for one year.

The Economic Dimension

In the section on trade and investment, some of the future areas of difficulty in Sino-American economic relations were considered. Although both sides have sought to alleviate the acute problems, there are still latent contentious issues. The Chinese are alarmed about American protectionism, impatient over slow technology transfers and concerned about the slow rate of American investment in China. On their side, American business people remain impatient with the often confusing results of economic reform, concerned over the slow and circuitous development of investment regulations and uneasy over periodic signs that China might be rethinking aspects of its "great leap outward."

What might be most ominous for the future of Sino-American economic relations is the frequent failure to think through the possible consequences of a fully reformed China for American interests. Recently *The Economist* (London) posed the following question: "Hold on. Does the West really want a stronger China?"

It is an obvious question, but one that is rarely addressed in depth. In our enthusiastic support for the reform leadership in China, we often do not think through the possible consequences of an economically strong China. There are, for example, valid national security reasons for considering technology transfer carefully. Moreover, American labor is showing growing concern over possible competition from China. As China's light industry continues to develop, it may well be looking for new markets for its television sets, bicycles and refrigerators. There are innumerable economic and strategic questions that would be raised by a China that continues on its current course or, perhaps, due to a changed political coalition, embarks on new policy directions. It is not too early to begin considering these questions.

All of this should remind us that China is, more than anything else, a system in transition. It is likely to remain so throughout the second decade of normalized Sino-American relations. The past years have seen important changes in China's foreign and domestic policies—the "independent foreign policy," the improvement in Sino-Soviet relations, the "open door policy," to mention only a few. The remainder of the second decade will reveal whether these policies can mature and become firm even as China's political leadership passes to a new generation. It will also show whether American policymakers can sustain a policy that will have the dynamism, flexibility and, above all, sensitivity to meet the complex challenges posed by a China in transition.

Talking It Over
A Note for Students and Discussion Groups

This issue of the HEADLINE SERIES, like its predecessors, is published for every serious reader, specialized or not, who takes an interest in the subject. Many of our readers will be in classrooms, seminars or community discussion groups. Particularly with them in mind, we present below some discussion questions—suggested as a starting point only—and references for further reading.

Discussion Questions

What are the major reasons for optimism when contemplating the future of Sino-American relations? for pessimism?

Can the Chinese army use modern U.S. weapons? Do Chinese leaders want them? What will be the consequences if the United States sells sophisticated arms to China?

Why did China break with the Soviet Union in the first place? Have their disagreements been resolved? What factors will influence future relations between the two countries?

What should American objectives be in regard to the Taiwan question? Can such objectives he reached even while maintaining cordial relations with China? If not, what should U.S. policy be?

Since the death of Mao Zedong, the Chinese government has reformed many of its economic practices. What are the factors promoting the success of such an experiment in China? What factors complicate the process?

Deng Xiaoping is attempting to install his successors in power before his death. Have other totalitarian or authoritarian leaders succeeded in arranging their succession before their deaths? Why is this such a difficult matter?

What factors will shape the future development of Sino-American economic relations? What are the major problem areas and issues that will have to be faced?

READING LIST

Barnett, A. Doak, *The Making of Foreign Policy in China: Structure and Process*. Boulder, Colo., Westview Press, 1985. The dean of American political scientists studying China examines the foreign policymaking process in Beijing. A unique study of individuals and institutions.

——————, and Clough, Ralph N., eds., *Modernizing China: Post-Mao Reform and Development*. Boulder, Colo., Westview Press, 1986. A series of essays by leading specialists on the reforms in post-Mao China. Political developments, military policy, economic reform, cultural policies and social trends are covered.

Bernstein, Richard, *From the Center of the Earth: The Search for the Truth About China*. Boston, Little, Brown, 1982. A probing look at human relationships in China and how they were damaged by the Cultural Revolution.

Butterfield, Fox, *China: Alive in the Bitter Sea*. New York, Times Books, 1982. A Western reporter examines the state of human freedom and choice in China after the post-Mao liberalization and finds much unhappiness.

Fairbank, John K., *Chinabound: A Fifty-year Memoir*. New York, Harper & Row, 1982. America's most prominent Sinologist recounts the important years of his career, shedding light on the beginnings of U.S. relations with the Chinese Communists and how he trained a new cadre of American China experts.

Garrett, Banning N., and Glaser, Bonnie S., *War and Peace: The Views From Moscow and Beijing.* Berkeley, Calif., The Institute of International Studies, University of California, Policy Papers in International Affairs, No. 20, 1984. The most up-to-date analysis of what the Sino-Soviet split has done to international security.

Goldstein, Steven, "Sino-American Relations: Building a New Consensus." *Current History,* September 1984.

Harding, Harry, ed., *China's Foreign Relations in the 1980s.* New Haven, Yale University Press, 1984. A collection of essays looking at post-Mao foreign policy from several angles.

Kim, Samuel S., ed., *China and the World: Chinese Foreign Policy in the Post-Mao Era.* Boulder, Colo., Westview Press, 1984. Also a good collection on this topic. Note in particular Steven I. Levine's "China and the United States: The Limits of Interaction."

Mathews, Jay, and Mathews, Linda, *One Billion: A China Chronicle.* New York, Random House, 1983. How China's unique underground society has opened cracks in the totalitarian government, affecting humor, sex, education and even foreign policy.

Mills, William deB., "Generational Change in China." *Problems of Communism,* November/December 1983.

Nathan, Andrew J., *Chinese Democracy.* New York, Knopf, 1985. A provocative look at the nature and limits of democracy in the Chinese context.

Pollack, Jonathan, *The Lessons of Coalition Politics: Sino-American Security Relations.* Santa Monica, Calif., Rand Corporation, R-3133-AF, February 1984. A declassified version of a report on the intricacies of China's developing military relationship with the United States.

Schell, Orville, *Watch Out for the Foreign Guests! China Encounters the West.* New York, Pantheon Books, 1980. An astute traveler follows Deng Xiaoping in America and makes his own journey through China in the heady days just after normalization.

Shambaugh, David L., *The Making of a Premier: Zhao Ziyang's Provincial Career.* Boulder, Colo., Westview Press, 1984. The first published study of the head of China's government.

Snow, Helen Foster, *My China Years: A Memoir.* New York, Morrow, 1984. One of the first American reporters to meet the Chinese Communists looks back. This helps explain her own early work and that of Edgar Snow, whose classic *Red Star Over China* should also be read.

Statement of Ownership, Management and Circulation

(Required by 39 U.S.C. 3685)

1a. Title of publication: Headline Series.

1b. Publication No: 00178780.

2. Date of filing: September 30, 1985.

3. Frequency of issue: Jan., March, May, Sept., Nov.

3a. No. of issues published annually: 5.

3b. Annual subscription price: $12.00.

4. Complete mailing address of known office of publication: Foreign Policy Association, 205 Lexington Ave., New York, N.Y. 10016.

5. Complete mailing address of the headquarters of general business offices of the publisher: Same.

6. Full names and complete mailing address of publisher, editor, and managing editor: Publisher—Foreign Policy Association, 205 Lexington Ave., New York, N.Y. 10016; Editor—Nancy Hoepli, FPA, 205 Lexington Ave., New York, N.Y. 10016.

7. Owner: (If owned by a corporation, its name and address must be stated and also immediately thereunder the names and addresses of stockholders owning or holding 1 percent or more of total amount of stock. If not owned by a corporation, the names and addresses of the individual owners must be given. If owned by a partnership or other unincorporated firm, its name and address, as well as that of each individual must be given. If the publication is published by a nonprofit organization, its name and address must be stated.) Foreign Policy Association, Inc., 205 Lexington Ave., New York, N.Y. 10016. No stockholders—a nonprofit organization.

8. Known bondholders, mortgagees, and other security holders owning or holding 1 percent or more of total amount of bonds, mortgages or other securities (If there are none, so state) None.

9. For Completion by Nonprofit Organizations Authorized to Mail at Special Rates (Section 423.12 DMM only): The purpose, function, and nonprofit status of this organization and the exempt status for Federal income tax purposes (1) has not changed during preceding 12 months.

10.	Extent and Nature of Circulation	Average No. Copies Each Issue During Preceding 12 Months	Actual Number of Copies of Single Issue Published Nearest to Filing Date
A.	Total no. copies (net press run)	15,872	14,490
B.	Paid and/or requested circulation		
	1. Sales through dealers and carriers, street vendors and counter sales	5,206	1,222
	2. Mail subscription (paid and/or requested)	5,838	4,622
C.	Total paid and/or requested circulation (Sum of 10B1 and 10B2)	11,044	5,568
D.	Free distribution by mail, carrier or other means Samples, complimentary, and other free copies	500	460
E.	Total distribution (Sum of C and D)	11,544	6,318
F.	Copies not distributed		
	1. Office use, left over, unaccounted, spoiled after printing	4,328	8,172
	2. Return from news agents	None	None
G.	Total (Sum of E, F1 and 2—should equal net press run shown in A)	15,872	14,490

11. I certify that the statements made by me above are correct and complete.

Mark Callahan

MARK CALLAHAN
Business Manager